SATOMI ICHIKAWA

Happy Birthday!

A Book of Birthday Celebrations

Text by Elizabeth Laird

Philomel Books
New York

© Editions Gautier-Languereau 1987
© American Edition Philomel Books 1988
First USA edition published in 1988 by
Philomel Books, a division of the Putnam Publishing Group,
51 Madison Avenue, New York NY 10010. All rights reserved.
No part of this publication may be reproduced, stored in a
retrieval system, or transmitted, in any form or by any means,
electronic, mechanical, photocopying, recording or otherwise,
without the prior permission of the publishers.
Printed and bound in Italy. First impression.

"Happy Birthday to You" by Mildred J. and Patty S. Hill
copyright © 1935 Birch Tree Group Ldt.
All rights reserved. Used by permission.

Library of Congress Cataloging-in-Publication Data
Ichikawa, Satomi. Happy Birthday.

Summary: Follows a year of different birthday celebrations
in a little girl's life and describes how birthdays
are celebrated around the world.
1. Birthdays - Juvenile literature. [1. Birthdays] I. Title
GT2430.I24   1987   394.2   87-11110
ISBN 0-399-21421-6

Contents

Birthdays

What do you like best about your birthday? Do you like having a party and inviting all your friends? Do you like finding a mysterious pile of parcels by your plate, and unwrapping them one by one? Or do you like that exciting feeling inside that tells you all day long that today is your own special day?

Birthdays come in all shapes and sizes. There are very important ones, like a first birthday, that celebrate the baby's first year of life, and the twenty-first birthday, when a person 'comes of age', or a hundredth birthday, when a person has lived for one whole century.

Every birthday's different, but every year the message is the same. We look back in wonder to the miracle of our birth, and look forward hopefully to happy days to come.

Birthdays are very special for everyone. For Julie, the little girl in this book, and her baby brother Peter, they are the best days of all . . .

A new baby

Have you ever seen a new born baby? Have you tickled its feet and watched its toes curl up? And have you seen it open its mouth, screw up its eyes and scream the house down when it's hungry?

Julie remembers the day when Peter was born. He was all red and crumpled, but very, very sweet. She and Daddy went into the garden and planted a plum tree. "Peter's tree," said Daddy. "We'll watch it grow like he grows."

A few months later, Peter was christened. He had two double chins, one curl of hair over each ear, and he looked like a serious old gentleman. "Just like his father!" said Aunt Lucy, who lived next door, and she gave him a great big teddy bear.

His godmother gave him a plate with rabbits on it. His godfather gave him a book of Bible stories to read when he was older. Granny gave him a set of twelve little spoons from her cabinet, and Julie gave him the silver spoon and fork she'd had when she was a baby.

Now Peter's got so many spoons he can invite all his friends to tea. Some of them aren't quite sure what spoons are for, but they're having a good time anyway!

A birthday book for Julie

Julie has been given a new birthday book. It has every date of the year in it, and under each date are some spaces, so that Julie can write in the birthdays of all her friends and each person in her family.

There are quite a few names in Julie's birthday book already. First of all, she put her own birthday in. There's a long, long time to wait until it comes round again. She won't be eight until the middle of winter. She's written in Mother's and Daddy's birthdays too. They'll be a little sooner, in the autumn. Now when's Aunt Lucy's birthday? And what about her friends, Jessica and Edward? Julie will have to remember to ask them. Peter's birthday is the easiest of all. It's very soon – next week in fact! And he's going to be exactly one year old.

Julie hasn't forgotten to take her birthday book when she meets her friends in the park.

"When's your birthday?" she asks Jessica.

"It's on Midsummer's day," says Jessica. "June 24."

"What about yours?" Julie asks Edward.

"It's on Midsummer's day too, silly," says Edward.

"Don't forget we're twins!"

11

Little Lamb, who made thee?

Little lamb, who made thee?
Dost thou know who made thee?
Gave thee life, and bid thee feed,
By the stream and over mead?
Gave thee clothing of delight,
Softest clothing, woolly, bright?
Gave thee such a tender voice,
Making all the vales rejoice?
Little lamb, who made thee?
Dost thou know who made thee?

Little lamb, I'll tell thee,
Little lamb, I'll tell thee:
He is called by thy name,
For he calls himself a lamb.
He is meek, and he is mild,
He became a little child.
I a child, and thou a lamb
We are called by his name.
Little lamb, God bless thee!
Little lamb, God bless thee!

William Blake

A spring birthday for Peter

Peter's going to be one year old tomorrow. Julie can hardly wait. She's bought him a big, red ball for his present, and she's going to make him a special birthday card.

"Aren't you excited, Peter?" she says.

But Peter just bounces up and down in his cot and shouts "Mama!"

He doesn't understand what all the fuss is about. He just wants Mother to come and give him some breakfast.

Clever cards

What is your favorite kind of birthday card? Do you like the funny ones with jokes inside, or do you like the pretty ones with beautiful pictures and poems?

Julie likes home-made cards best. Before she starts work, she gets together all the things she's going to need: sheets of thin white cardboard, scissors, a ruler, some crayons, pens, pencils, scraps of colored paper and cloth, and paste.

First, she measures out squares on the big sheet of cardboard, and draws lines to mark them off, so that when she cuts out the birthday cards they will be the right size and shape. (She usually asks Mother to check that she's got it right before she starts cutting.) Then, she cuts them out, and folds them in half.

Now the real fun begins, as Julie thinks of how to decorate them. Sometimes she sticks bits of paper on the front to make an interesting collage. Sometimes she just draws a picture, colors it in, and writes a friendly birthday greeting inside.

Sometimes Julie makes a peep-show card. She cuts out a shape in the front part so that the middle can be seen. Then she draws a picture on the inside page so that part of it can be seen through the hole.

For very special cards, Julie makes clever surprises. The card she's made for Peter has a flower on the front, with a center that opens out. Her birthday message is written inside the flower. Of course, she'll have to read it for Peter. He can't read yet. But he's going to have a lot of fun, opening and shutting the flower!

Cut a small square of paper and fold the four corners to the center. Stick it on the front of a card and draw a flower around it. Now write your birthday message inside, and close it up again.

Draw a heart on the front of the card, and carefully cut it out. Draw around your hand on the cut-out piece and then color it. Stick it on the inside page so you can see it through the hole.

←FOLD→

Draw the picture on the front, then cut through both layers of card together. Be careful not to cut the folded side!

Draw a house on the front and color it. Snip around the windows and draw little pictures or write messages on the inside. Be careful not to cut the folding side.

The birthday song

Words and Music by MILDRED J. HILL
and PATTY S. HILL
Arranged by BONNIE GREENE

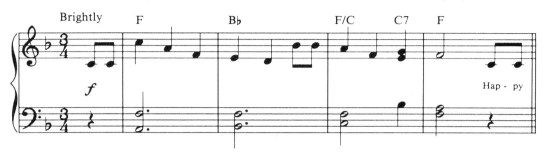

Everyone knows the "Happy Birthday" song. It's sung in Chile and China, Ireland and India, New York and New Zealand. It was written about 90 years ago by two American ladies, Mildred and Patty Hill.

Even if it's not your birthday just yet, why don't you sing it?

16

There's just one candle on the cake for a boy who's one today. Peter wanted to pull it out of the cake and play with it.

"No," says Mother. "It will burn you if you touch it. You have to blow it out."

Peter tries, but he doesn't know how to blow. None of his friends can help him. They're too busy playing with his new toys, or chewing the wrapping paper, or wondering when they're going to get a piece of cake. Perhaps Julie will show him how to blow. Or maybe Aunt Lucy will help.

17

"What were birthdays like when you were young?" Julie asks Aunt Lucy.

18

The old lady smiles, "Oh we had a lot of fun, just like you."

A birthday in Scandinavia

Astrid is a lucky girl. Her birthday is on May 17th, which is Norway's birthday too. There'll be all kinds of celebrations today throughout the land, and the whole family will wear their national costume.

Mother has baked a special marzipan cake. It's made of whipped egg white, ground almonds and icing sugar, baked in rings and joined with burnt sugar. It's covered with whirls of white icing. Later on, Astrid will decorate it with Norwegian flags.

"It's time to get up, Astrid! You're going to have a very busy day."

A midsummer birthday for the twins

Summer has come at last, and the twins will soon be seven. Julie opens her party invitation. What a surprise! Edward and Jessica are having a fancy dress party!

Now Julie will be busy. She's got to make presents for the twins, and think of a costume for herself. And the twins have got to decorate the garden for the party, help prepare the food, and plan all the party games. Only two weeks left to go!

Gorgeous gifts

Summery presents are easy to make. There are bright-colored flowers in the garden, ideal for making Victorian posies. There is lavender, too, that can be used for stuffing sweet-smelling lavender bags, made out of pretty scraps of cotton or silk. When you keep them in a drawer among your clothes, everything you wear will smell sweet and fresh.

Summer fruits, too, can be presented in attractive ways. Decorate some cardboard with your own painted or crayoned pattern, make it into a little basket, and fill it with fruit. The fruit has to be eaten at once, but the basket can be kept for storing little treasures.

Summer is the season for growing things too. Pansies, petunias, and all kinds of bright-colored flowers will grow happily on a window sill, and your friends will remember you every time they water your gift.

Julie had to plan ahead for some of her presents. The flower seeds had to be planted and watered, and it's taken months for them to grow. The lavender needed to be cut and dried before it could be used.

Some presents, though, have to be quickly made and quickly given. The posy of flowers must be given while it's fresh and pretty. And the cherries in the basket are just asking to be eaten!

Pot plants Paint an old yogurt pot with oil based paint. Make a few holes in the bottom, and put in some small stones. Fill the pot with moist earth and plant flower seeds. Pansies and petunias are fun to grow. Keep your plants in a sunny place, and water regularly.

A posy. Cut a hole in a round piece of paper and cut a lacy pattern

around the edge. Strip the leaves off the stems of the flowers, push them through the central hole, and arrange flowers neatly. Tie a ribbon around the stem. Keep the stems in water until you present the posy.

Lavender bags. Strip the flowers off some dried lavender heads. Fold a rectangle of pretty material in half and sew up the sides to make a bag. Fill it with lavender and sew up the top and tie it with a ribbon.

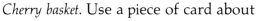

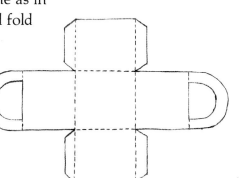

Cherry basket. Use a piece of card about 8 × 12 ins. Draw an outline as in the picture. Cut it out and fold along all the lines. Glue the side flaps and stick them inside the basket. Line the basket with clear plastic wrap and fill with cherries.

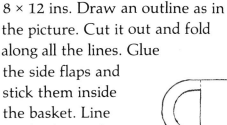

Pretty paper

Red paper, yellow paper, blue paper, green paper and paper with patterns all over it – which do you like best?

Julie is making her own wrapping paper. She started off with some plain white and colored tissue papers, some poster paint, a small knife (a paring knife), and a few potatoes and carrots that she's using to make prints with.

First, she washed the potatoes and carrots, and cut them in half. Then, she made the shapes she wanted by carving around the cut ends of the vegetables. (She was careful not to cut her fingers!)

Next, she dipped the vegetables in paint and pressed them onto some old newspaper to see if they made clear enough patterns. They were beautiful! Her hearts, flowers, fish and stars looked wonderfully bright.

Now she's ready to start on the tissue paper. She presses her potato and carrot shapes onto the paper to make lovely colorful patterns.

What shapes would you like to make? You could do the sky at night, with the moon and stars, or autumn leaf shapes in orange and yellow, or jazzy triangles, squares and circles, or brilliant butterflies and summery flowers.

Some parcels are easy to wrap, and some are harder, but a present that's a really tricky shape is simpler to wrap if you put it in a box first. Fold the paper around the box and stick the edges down with sticky cellophane tape.

Pick a ribbon to match the color of the paper. An easy way to make a pretty bow is to tie a knot, then make one loop, tape that down and make another, tape that down, and so on until you have a big bow.

Julie has remembered to label her presents clearly. She had to write quite small to get all the words on.

What a tempting pile of presents!

Dainty decorations

Jessica made these lovely paper chains. For the first one she made little bows out of squares of tissue paper and strung them together on a length of colored wool. To make the chain look more attractive she lightly glued the corners of each bow to the next one.

For the second kind of chain Jessica used some leftover wallpaper. She cut it into 6-inch squares then cut each square into 6 strips. She pasted the first strip into a circle and then looped the next through it, and so on until she had a long chain.

For the third and fourth kinds of chains, she used colored construction paper, folded and cut as shown in the pictures.

Edward made the lanterns. He folded sheets of paper in half, cut slits in them, then unfolded them and glued them down the side. They look beautiful hanging from a paper streamer.

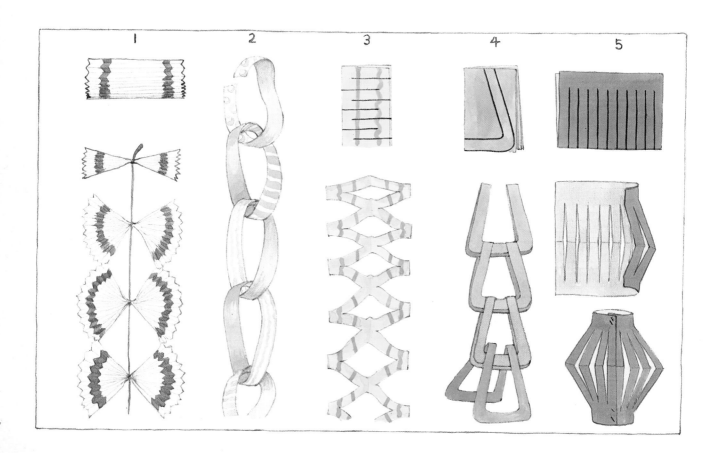

And now for the finishing touches! Up go the streamers, the paper chains and the Japanese lanterns. Edward is fixing a "Welcome" sign on the garden gate, and he is tying a bunch of balloons to the gatepost to help the young guests find the right house.

It would certainly be strange if anyone got lost. You could hardly walk past this house without realizing that something special was going on!

WELCOME

Fabulous food

You can't have a birthday party without a birthday cake! The twins are making a sandwich cake, in two halves. Here's the recipe:

For the cake
½ cup (4 ounces) soft margarine
½ cup granulated sugar
2 eggs
rind of one lemon
1 teaspoon lemon juice
½ cup of wholemeal flour
1 teaspoon baking powder

For the icing
1¼ cups confectioners sugar
lemon juice
cocoa

Heat the oven to 350 degrees F. Grease two 8-inch round layer cake pans. Beat the margarine with an electric beater or a wooden spoon until it is soft. Add the sugar, and go on beating until the mixture is pale and fluffy. Beat in the eggs, one at a time, and add the grated rind of the lemon and a teaspoon of lemon juice. Then beat in the flour and the baking powder. Divide the mixture between the cake pans, and bake for about 25 minutes until the cakes are golden brown. Cool on a wire rack. Make the icing by mixing the sifted icing sugar with the lemon juice, a little at a time, until it is the right consistency for spreading. Ice the cakes as evenly as you can. Mix some extra icing with cocoa to make the bow tie. Decorate with chocolate buttons, nuts, orange slices and raisins.

Fresh things taste good on a hot summer's day. Edward loves the soft rolls filled with mashed banana or honey. Each one is wrapped in its own little bag.

Jessica wants to nibble the crunchy, crisp salad titbits. Everyone's going to love the fresh fruit salad, a mixture of melon, oranges, pears, strawberries and grapes served up in a watermelon basket. There are two kinds of cool drinks: fresh orange juice and a fruit punch.

This spiky hedgehog is a cake too. It was made with the ingredients opposite. The two rounds were cut in half and sandwiched together with jam. The cake stands upright and is covered with chocolate icing. Chocolate sticks make the prickles.

Delightful Disguises

Cat

King

Ballerina

Clown

Chef

Peter Pan

Space Man

Charlie Chaplin

Cowboy

Scarecrow

Pierrot

Harlequin

Medieval Queen

Statue of Liberty

Native American

Rajah

Robot

Indian Woman

Pirate

Funny faces

Finish off your fancy dress by painting a fancy face. You could even manage without a costume if your make-up is good enough. A moustache and beard will turn you into a dashing cavalier or a handsome king. Some horrible green shadows and cleverly added wrinkles will make you look like a wicked old witch, while a few whiskers and a black nose will turn you into a friendly purry cat.

If you want to be more adventurous, try to copy some of the faces on this page, but be careful to use proper face paints or make-up. Ordinary paint, felt-tip pens or crayons might hurt your skin. And remember, it's best not to put anything too near your eyes. It can be painful when you try to get it off again.

Have fun, and see if your friends will recognize you!

Hilarious hi-jinks

Hoppy balloons

You need two teams for this. One person from each team puts a balloon between his or her knees and jumps around the course. The next person starts as soon as the first one finishes and touches him or her. Each player takes a turn. First team to finish is the winner.

The tightrope

Lay a rope along the ground, and walk along it. If your other foot touches the ground you're out. The one who gets to the end with the fewest wobbles wins.

A throwing game

Make a pyramid of empty cans and stand behind a line ten paces away. Try to knock the cans down with a soft ball.

A shooting game

Set up a row of lighted candles stuck in empty flower pots and try to shoot them out with a water pistol.

Fishing for surprises

This game takes a little longer to prepare, but it is great fun. Wrap up some small presents, and tie them with string. To make a fishing rod, tie a string to a stick, and attach a hook to the end of it. Now get your friends to fish the little packets out with it. What will they find inside?

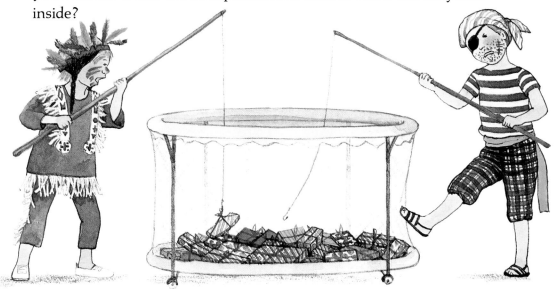

After all the hard work, it's party time at last. "Come on everyone! Food's ready!" calls the clown. Only a few people have heard him. The others are too busy running around and playing games.

They'd better be quick, or the jugs of delicious cool drinks, the piles of fruit, the lollipop sticks, the platefuls of tasty rolls and the bowlfuls of fruit salad will disappear into other hungry, little mouths.

The Echoing Green

… The skylark and thrush,
The birds of the bush,
Sing louder around,
To the bells' cheerful sound,
While our sports shall be seen
On the Echoing Green.

… Till the little ones, weary,
No more can be merry;
The sun does descend,
And our sports have an end.
Round the laps of their mothers
Many sisters and brothers
Like birds in their nest,
Are ready for rest,
And sport no more seen
On the darkening Green.

from *The Echoing Green* by William Blake

A harvest birthday for Mother

It's autumn already. Mother's birthday comes next. How can Julie make it a wonderful day? She can't afford to buy Mother an expensive present, or take her out to a restaurant.

"I know," says Julie. "Mother works so hard every day she'd like a rest on her birthday. That gives me an idea ..."

On this important morning, Julie is up bright and early and ready to get started. She helped Daddy to get the breakfast ready, and he carried Mother's up to her on a tray. Now she's washing the dishes.

"What next, Julie?" says Daddy.

"We'll do the dusting and sweeping," says Julie, who has worked everything out, "and Peter can pick some flowers."

"And then?" smiles Daddy.

"And then, please Daddy, can you help me to make Mother's birthday cake? I know just how I want to do it, but I need you to help me find the ingredients and put the oven on."

"What kind of cake is it going to be?" says Daddy.

"That's a secret," says Julie. "You'll just have to wait and see."

Daddy smiles.

A cake for Mother

Julie's made a chocolate heart for Mother. She used the same recipe the twins used (page 28) but instead of putting in lemon juice and rind, she mixed two tablespoonfuls of cocoa with a little cold water to make a smooth paste, and beat it into the cake mixture. When the cake was cooked and cooled, she sandwiched the halves together with black cherry jam and cut it into a heart shape.

To make the icing, Julie melted 3½ ounces of unsweetened baking chocolate in a bowl over hot water, and stirred in the juice of an orange, a tablespoon of sugar and a teaspoon of cooking oil. She poured this mixture over the cake. It was thick and shiny and smelled delicious. When the chocolate had set, she decorated the cake with walnuts.

"How many candles shall I put on it, Daddy?" she asked.

"Just put one on," said Daddy. "Mother might prefer to keep her age a secret!"

What a lot of visitors! Julie's heart beats a little faster as she brings on the birthday cake.

But everyone's delighted.
"It's beautiful, darling," gasps
Mother. "I can't wait to try it!"

A birthday tradition in Japan

In Japan, some birthdays matter more than others. Girls who have had their third or seventh birthday during the year, and boys who have had their fifth, go to the shrine on November 15th. There, they give thanks to God for their health and strength, and pray for a long life to come. This tradition comes from long ago when many children died before their third, fifth or seventh birthday. After the shrine a family feast is held at home.

This ceremony, called the "Seven, five, three", is the day for wearing your best kimono, and, if you're a girl, a ribbon in your hair. The biggest treat, perhaps, is a trip to buy special bags of candies with the words "Sweets for 1000 years of life" written on them.

An autumn birthday for Daddy

It's Daddy's birthday today! Now what kind of treat would he like best? Julie and Mother have put their heads together. As soon as Daddy has gone to work, they're going to start preparing the surprise. They know what would please Daddy most ...

Daddy comes home to a surprise birthday dinner, with candles and flowers and all the trimmings. And he's going to share it with Mother and the children, the people he loves most in the world. Do you think he'll open his presents before or after dinner? And what do you think is inside that long parcel?

The long parcel was a fishing rod! Just what Daddy wanted! And on Saturday afternoon, Julie and Daddy go off to the river to try it out.

"We're going to catch a salmon!" shouts Julie. "And a trout! And a big fat pike! And we'll have them for dinner with french fries!"

Daddy laughs.

"We might be lucky," he says, "and then again, we might not, but I don't mind if we don't catch anything at all. It's fun just going out together."

First birthdays in Africa

All over Africa, in the jungles, and deserts, in the great cities, and on the high grasslands, people celebrate with joy the birth of a baby.

In the deep forests of Gabon, the Pygmy mother sings a birth-song to her child. In Kenya, the Masai mother takes her baby on her back, and goes to the thorn enclosure where the precious cattle are kept. There, her husband waits with the village elders, and there standing among the cows, the child is given his name.

Shouts echo across the mountains of Ethiopia, sending news of a baby's birth: five shouts for a boy, and three for a girl.

In the hot, busy cities of West Africa, the old ceremony of "outdooring" is still held. When the baby is eight days old, her mother takes her out of the house for her first look at the big, wide world, and friends and family are invited to meet her.

In Eygpt, there's a procession on the seventh day of the baby's life. Children dance ahead with flowers and candles, and sing this song:

> "Birgalatak, Birgalatak,
> Golden ear-rings brightly dangling,
> O God bless him, may he grow up
> And run hither, and play thither
> Up and down the house all over.
> Birgalatak, Birgalatak!"

A winter birthday for Julie

And now the big day is nearly here, the one that Julie's been waiting for all through the year. It's her very own birthday tomorrow. What will those mysteriously wrapped parcels contain? What will her friends think of her party dress? What will it feel like to be eight years old at last?

The birthday album

Every year, since she was born, Daddy has taken photographs of Julie on her birthday. Now she's arranging them all in one big album. What fun it will be when she's grown up to look back at all her birthdays. She's starting a new page in the album for this year's birthday pictures and Daddy's put a fresh film in his camera all ready for the big day.

Birthstones and flowers

Did you know that you have a birthstone?

There are many old beliefs about stones. In the middle ages, people believed that diamonds protected you from evil, and that pearls and sapphires were good medicines against poison.

You've got a birthday flower, too. See if you can find it on the chart.

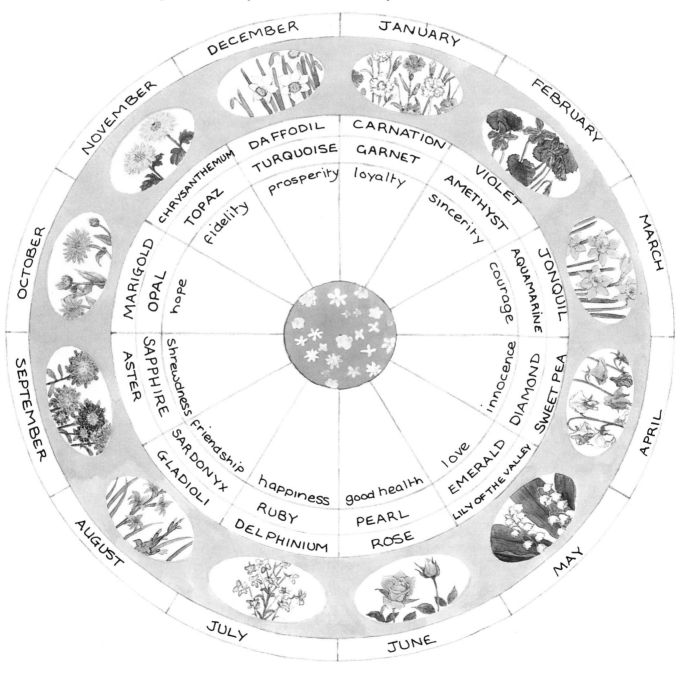

Birthdays in the stars

Do you know your Zodiac sign? In the olden days people looked up at the night sky and imagined animal shapes in the arrangements of the stars. They gave these shapes names, and called them the signs of the Zodiac ("Zodiac" comes from a Greek word that means "living things"). They believed that people's lives could be affected by the stars. Some people still believe that.

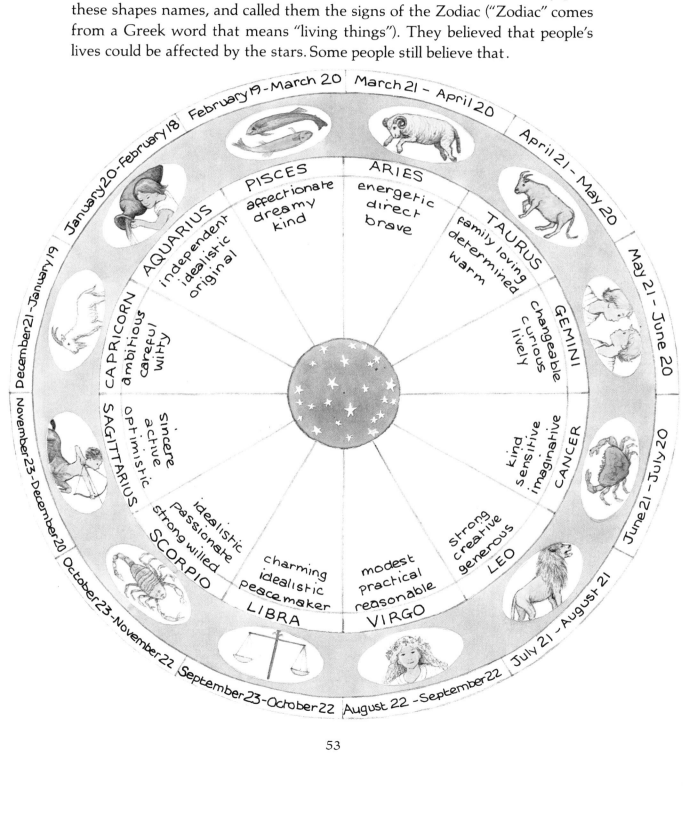

The birthday girl

Here comes the birthday girl, peeping through the banisters! She was so excited last night she couldn't go to sleep, but now that the great day is here at last she's suddenly feeling rather shy. Everyone's looking at her and singing, "Happy birthday!"

"Ju-ju!" shouts Peter. He can't say "Julie" very well. He doesn't understand about birthdays, but he knows there's something exciting going on, and he wants to be the first to give Julie a big hug when she comes down for breakfast.

And what a breakfast it is! There are eggs, and piles of delicious warm buns, and even croissants, decorated with the first early flowers from the garden. And Mother's put out the best china, with Julie's favorite plate at her place, and a pretty birthday card from all the family. She'll get her presents later on today. Aunt Lucy's giving her a new dress to wear at the party. She knows about that already. But what will her friends give her when they come to the party? And what will Mother and Daddy give her? That's going to be the nicest surprise of all.

"Now young lady," says Daddy, when breakfast is over, "we've got a job to do."

"I know," says Julie. "You've got to measure me to see if I've grown since last year, and make a new mark on the wall."

Julie stands against the wall, while Daddy measures her. She's done it every year since she was a baby. Julie has to keep her feet together and stand very straight. She wants to be as tall as possible.

Peter wonders what the stick thing is that Daddy's got, and why he's put it on Julie's head. He wants to have a turn, too. "Three feet nine inches," says Daddy. "You've grown nearly two inches in a year. Well done, Julie!"

Wow! What a noise! There's no doubt that everyone's enjoying themselves. You could hear their screams of delight miles away. The party's certainly going full swing.

Whose turn is it to put the blindfold on and try to pin the tail on the donkey? No one's got anywhere near it yet. Perhaps Julie herself will win the prize.

It's time for refreshments, and here comes Julie's birthday cake. The cake bits are sandwiched between layers of cream and fudgy icing and it's decorated with kiwi fruit and oranges.

It's a good thing it's such a big cake. It looks so good that everyone's going to want a very large slice.

"Me first! Me first!" shouts one of Julie's friends.

"No," says another. "The birthday girl gets the first piece."

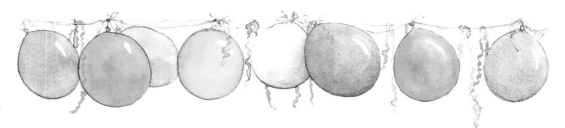

A birthday wish

The candles are lit, and Julie makes a wish. What is she wishing for? A doll's house? A pair of skates? A bicycle? No, she's thinking of something quite different, something warm and furry and very much alive. More than anything else in the world, Julie wants a real, live pet of her very own.

"Come on, blow the candles out!" the others say. They can't wait for the cake to be cut.

Julie takes a deep breath. If she blows them all out at once, perhaps her wish will come true.

"Whoosh!"

Oh dear, the last one's still lit. But Julie's seen it, and with her last tiny puff of breath she blows it out. She's done it!

A wish come true

Julie's wish has come true! Her birthday present is a puppy, a wriggling, tail wagging, barking, licking, bouncing, jumping, furry little puppy. Julie is so happy she picks him up at once, and the puppy seems to smile.

"I know what," says Julie. "I'll call you 'Smiley'."

Smiley wriggles so much that Julie has to put him down.

"Think of all the fun we're going to have," says Julie, "all the romps, and chases, and games of hide and seek. I'm going to take you for your very first walk tomorrow, down by the river to see the ducks."

Smiley wags his tails so hard that half his body wags too. Peter tries to copy him. He's a lot like a little puppy himself really.

"We're going to be best friends," says Julie, picking Smiley up again and giving him a gentle hug.

"I just know we are. Best friends for ever and ever."